The Attic, The Pearls & Three Fine Girls

The Attic, the Pearls & Three Fine Girls

JENNIFER BREWIN, LEAH CHERNIAK, ANN-MARIE MACDONALD,
ALISA PALMER AND MARTHA ROSS

The Attic, The Pearls & Three Fine Girls
first published 1999 by
Scirocco Drama
An imprint of J. Gordon Shillingford Publishing Inc.
© 1999 Brewin, Cherniak, MacDonald, Palmer and Ross

Scirocco Drama Series Editor: Dave Carley
Cover design by Terry Gallagher/Doowah Desigh Inc.
Printed and bound in Canada

Published with the financial assistance of The Canada Council for the Arts and
the Manitoba Arts Council

Canadian Cataloguing in Publication Data

The attic, the pearls & three fine girls

A play.
ISBN 1-896239-50-1

I. Brewin, Jennifer

PS8500.A88 1999   C812'.54   C99-900656-8
PR9199.3.A753 1999

For all the sisters.

Jennifer Brewin, Leah Cherniak, Alisa Palmer, Ann-Marie MacDonald, Martha Ross

About the Authors

Jennifer Brewin has worked as a freelance director and producer. She is the co-artistic director of the Caravan Farm Theatre in British Columbia.

Leah Cherniak is co-artistic director of Theatre Columbus in Toronto. Besides directing and performing for other theatres across Canada, Leah has directed, co-created and/or performed in over twenty new Canadian plays produced by Theatre Columbus. Her daughter Margaret inspired major changes in the text of *The Attic, The Pearls & Three Fine Girls* and continues to inspire her life.

Ann-Marie MacDonald is a writer and actor. Her works include the play *Goodnight Desdemona (Good Morning Juliet)* and the novel, *Fall on Your Knees*.

Alisa Palmer is a director and writer. Currently the artistic director of Nightwood Theatre, she is also a freelance director who works across Canada. Among her works is the Chalmers Award-winning *A Play About the Mothers of Plaza de Mayo*.

Martha Ross attended the Jacques LeCoq School in Paris, and has been acting and writing for her company Theatre Columbus since she founded it with Leah Cherniak in 1983. She is currently writing a play with music (in collaboration with her husband John Millard) about three Canadians stranded in a snow storm.

Notes on the Characters

JOJO is an untenured English professor in her early forties. Somewhat dowdy, she seethes with suppressed passions. She likes to think of herself as the wise and benevolent eldest sister, but she is hyper-sensitive and given to sudden displays of histrionics.

JAYNE is a successful Bay Street shark, and a severely closeted lesbian. JAYNE is the middle child. She believes there is no problem that cannot be solved using a flow chart, and deludes herself that her emotions are under strict control. She is, in fact, a ferocious marshmallow.

JELLY is the youngest, a self-employed, self-supporting artist. Despite her sisters' beliefs, JELLY is not only a serious artist, she is revealed as the most responsible and pragmatic of the three. She sympathizes with and loves her sisters, and is tortured by the battle that rages between them. She is very tolerant but, in the end, she can only be pushed so far...

Production History

The Attic, The Pearls & Three Fine Girls was first produced by Theatre Columbus in Toronto at the Theatre Centre West in Spring 1995. It was subsequently reworked, and remounted by Theatre Columbus in Toronto with Buddies in Bad Times Theatre in Spring 1997. In Winter 1998, Great Canadian Theatre Company produced it in Ottawa with the original company. Several other productions have followed.

JOJO Fine .... Martha Ross
JAYNE Fine .... Ann-Marie MacDonald
JELLY Fine .... Leah Cherniak

Directed by Alisa Palmer
Associate Artist: Jennifer Brewin
Set, Costumes, Props Design by Dany Lyne
Lighting Design by Andrea Lundy
Original Music by Allen Cole & John Millard
Vocals by John Millard
Sound Design by Cathy Nosaty (second two productions)
Stage Manager: Ellen Flowers (first production)
Stage Manager: Sharon DiGenova (second two productions)

Preface

From a pearl, a suitcase and some nostalgic party tunes emerged a story of three sisters who are as inextricably linked as three grown women can be. Welcome to *The Attic, The Pearls & Three Fine Girls*. This raucous and moving comedy sprang from the desire of three performers to work together. Via improvisation, it quickly grew into the story of three sisters who can't leave each other—or well enough—alone.

Reunited on the occasion of their father's death, Jojo, Jayne and Jelly are three freshly orphaned adults who still have some serious reckoning to do with the past and each other. There is a great deal of love amongst these sisters. And as much anger and sorrow. The three shared an intensely private and imaginative world growing up. They reprise that intensity as well as their delight, as they battle both to reclaim one another and redefine themselves. This is where the comedy comes from—good intentions gone awry, anger seething beneath a veneer of maturity and independence, not to mention the final irony of the "irresponsible" youngest sister turning out to be the foundation of the new family order.

The Attic, The Pearls & Three Fine Girls was built to be performed in an hour and a half with no intermission. Fast and precise, the comedy is as physical as it verbal, yet it is essential never to sacrifice the emotional truth of the story—though they strive to conceal it, the stakes are high for these sisters from the first moment, and the stakes continue to build until the final attic scene. Their readiness to flip from tears to laughter, from complicity to conflict, is what fuels the comedy. And when the gloves come off, there is no blow too low…

The old family house is almost as much a character as the sisters themselves. It's a musty, eccentric home full of overstuffed armchairs, gewgaws, tchotchkes and knicknacks, although nothing is purely decorative. Every object in the room feels as though it could be redolent with sentimental meaning. The set for the house must also accomodate many different places—a living room, kitchen, graveside and attic. We accomplished this by having large windows that moved, a kitchen table that flew in and out, a trap door that appeared from the floor (or the wall depending on the theatre) and three trunks full of old dresses and pertinent objects that were opened or shut depending on the scene.

The music, both the original themes composed for the play, and the familiar old party tunes, makes up a fifth character. It is present in very specific and critical moments in the play. The opening theme, a brooding, sensual groove, recurs during Jojo's sexual fantasies in the attic, and again in the last torture scene amongst the sisters. The heartfelt ballad that drives the funeral sequence is reprised at the only other brief moment of tranquility amongst the sisters at the end of the play. A delicately ominous sustained note which appears with Mum's pearls reinforces this object's mysterious power. The music, warm, dark, intensely angry, hilariously funny and lovingly paternal, tells a great deal about what is at the heart of the play. Listening to the original score is well worth the time of anyone planning to perform the play, as it provides an entirely emotional and inarticulable sense of the world of the Fine sisters.

The Attic, The Pearls & Three Fine Girls is a story full of ferocious love in all its disguises: anger, resentment, jealousy, loss and overwhelming joyful complicity. We hope you enjoy your visit with the Fine girls. You may even find them surprisingly familiar…!

Alisa Palmer
Director and Co-Writer

Prologue

The Past

(Music. Playful yet driving and intense. Lights up on the attic. In the centre of the room, JOJO stands atop a trunk, resplendant in an outsized ballgown; this is the coveted garment that the sisters refer to as "the torture dress". JOJO plays a tambourine fiercely, passionately. JAYNE, dressed in a tuxedo several sizes too big for her and wearing a pink turban on her head, dances and whirls wildly, a long strand of pearls flying about her neck. JAYNE obeys all of JOJO's commands.)

JOJO: Dance! Dance, my sister, dance until you die! Stop. Do the twist. Stop. Do the monkey. Stop. Kneel before me. Now...who do you love the most?

JAYNE: You, your majesty.

JOJO: Why, pray tell?

JAYNE: Because you are the oldest and also the wisest.

JOJO: And?

JAYNE: And the ugliest.

JOJO: Jayne!

JAYNE: And the most beautiful of all the Fine sisters—okay Jojo, I want to wear the torture dress now.

JOJO: No! I am wearing the torture dress and I shall decide when and if you ever get to wear it. Come to think of it, give me Mum's pearls.

JAYNE: No, I get to wear Mum's pearls this time, you said, 'cause you got to wear the torture dress—!

            (Their scuffle is interrupted by a thumping sound from the trunk under JOJO's feet. Muffled cries. JOJO and JAYNE giggle.)

JOJO: Who is it?

JELLY: *(From inside trunk.)* It's me, Jelly!

JAYNE: *(To the trunk.)* Is your refrigerator running?

JELLY: Let me out!

JOJO: We can't, Jelly, you have to have your nap.

JAYNE: Babies need naps.

            (A yowl from JELLY. JOJO and JAYNE open the trunk. JELLY climbs out, wailing. She is wearing dress-ups including a giant pointy brassiere over her clothes, and clutches a battered teddy bear.)

JOJO: Oh Jelly, we were just teasing you.

JAYNE: Yeah, Jelly.

JELLY: *I'm telling!*

JOJO: You can wear the torture dress, Jelly.

JELLY: No!

JAYNE: Jelly, do you want to wear Mum's pearls?

JELLY: We're not allowed to wear Mum's pearls, ever ! And you're not supposed to put me in *boxes*, Dad said—

JOJO &
JAYNE: "Dad *said!*"

JELLY: Stop it!

            (But JAYNE continues taunting JELLY with "Dad

said! Dad said!" over JELLY's protestations until JELLY seizes JAYNE's arm and bites it. JAYNE cries out in pain. She and JOJO are shocked.)

JAYNE: Jelly! No biting!

JOJO: Jelly! You must never bite!

JELLY: *(Stricken, no longer wailing, but weeping now and heartbroken.)* You hurt my feelings.

            (JELLY climbs back into the trunk, heartbroken. The sisters relent.)

JAYNE: Jelly? Want to play hunt-the-thimble?

JELLY: No.

JOJO: Want to play tea party, Jelly? You can be Mum. Here.

            (JOJO takes the pearls from JAYNE and puts them on JELLY who is suddenly content.)

JELLY: I'm Mum.

JAYNE: And you can invite anyone you like.

JELLY: I want to invite Mr Jones and his little wee dog.

JAYNE &
JOJO: Ooooo, Mr Jones and his little wee dog, little wee dog!

            (All three giggle wickedly, uncontrollably and begin dancing around the trunk chanting, "Little wee dog, Little wee dog!" until they are stopped by a knocking from the attic door.)

ALL: It's Dad!

            (They scramble out of their dress-ups, putting them and the pearls into the trunk. JOJO coaches JELLY, "We didn't wear Mum's pearls." They repeat the phrase in a whisper, giggling. Music and lights cue

a transition as JAYNE and JOJO exit, leaving JELLY alone with her teddy bear. The space transforms into the living room, many years later, and JELLY changes with it, from scampering child to grown woman. Music ends. JELLY looks over her shoulder toward door leading offstage, then she goes to the phone and dials.)

JELLY: It's Dad. I think you better come home.

                (JELLY picks up her old teddy bear and exits.)

Scene 1
Living Room

> (Grown-up JOJO enters. She wears a hairy tweed skirt, battered pumps, glasses, her hair arranged in some absent attempt at a bun. She appears perfectly composed at first, but gives way to a sudden noisy spasm of grief. She attempts to recover as JAYNE enters. JAYNE is smartly dressed for Bay and/or Wall Street—heels, jacket, skirt. JAYNE tactfully, if awkwardly, turns away from JOJO, repressing her own grief. After several embarrassed attempts, the two finally succeed in catching one another's eye, at which point they cross purposefully to each other and meet in a heartfelt embrace.)

JOJO: Oh Jayne…

JAYNE: Yuh.

JOJO: Yuh.

JAYNE: Yuh.

> (They pat each other's backs intently, several times too often, while repeating JAYNE's aspirated "yuh". They part finally to face one another. An awkward beat.)

JOJO: We should see each other more often.

JAYNE: I'd like that.

> (JAYNE goes to the bar, pours herself a Scotch. Throughout, these two are a little too quick to agree, a little to ready to smile at one another. In short, they are trying too hard, and we sense the tension of their estrangement.)

JOJO: It's just—he's so weak…

JAYNE: I know, I don't know if he even understands a word I say.

JOJO: It's that awful machine he's hooked up to.

JAYNE: At least he's here at home.

JOJO: At least he's not in some horrible hospital room.

          (JAYNE nods in agreement. A beat. They have run out of conversation.)

JAYNE: Where's Jelly?

JOJO: She's been in there for ages.

JAYNE: *(Imitating Dad.)* "Where the hell is Jell?"

          (They share a nostalgic chuckle, but quickly become choked up. Another awkward beat.)

JOJO: Thank goodness for Jelly.

JAYNE: Oh yeah, she's been a real trooper, moving back home, looking after Dad.

JOJO: *(Pleasantly.)* To tell you the truth, Jayne, I think she was just as happy to get out of that apartment of hers.

JAYNE: *(Equally pleasant.)* Well you know it makes sense for Jelly to look after Dad, what with her being unemployed.

JOJO: It's not that she's unemployed, Jayne, it's just that artists have more…free time.

JAYNE: Whatever.

          (Beat.)

JOJO: Won't be long now. You would think we'd be ready for it.

JAYNE: Well yeah, you'd think after—what—six months.

JOJO: Nine, really.

JAYNE: Nine, really.

> *(JELLY enters. She wears clothes that are partly of her own design. Not necessarily bizarre, but colourful and certainly in contrast to the conservative JAYNE and the tweedy JOJO.)*

JELLY: Hi.

JOJO: Oh Jelly—

JAYNE: It's okay, Jelly—

> *(JAYNE and JOJO cross to JELLY and embrace her. More backpatting. JELLY tries to speak but her sisters cut her off.)*

JOJO: I know, I know, Jelly—

JAYNE: I know, I know—

JOJO: It's okay—

JAYNE: It's okay—

JOJO: I know—

> *(JELLY walks away from them. JOJO and JAYNE don't miss a beat.)*

JAYNE: I know, it's hard for all of us, seeing him this way.

JOJO: I know. I can't even—I said, "Dad?" And he just sort of... *(Demonstrates a squeaking sound.)*

JAYNE: I know, it's so weird, you can hardly hear his voice; the man who never shut up.

JOJO: *(Jovially.)* "Vini, vidi, vici."

JAYNE: "Omne trinum est perfectum."

(JAYNE and JOJO's chuckles turn to stifled tears just as JELLY starts laughing. JOJO and JAYNE are puzzled.)

JELLY: He remembered the punch line.

JOJO: Who?

JELLY: Dad. He could never remember, "What's the difference between a pig and a lawyer? Pigs don't act like lawyers when they get drunk." *(Chuckling.)* He just sat right up and said it.

JAYNE: He spoke?

JELLY: Yes.

JAYNE: Just now?

JOJO: Did he say anything else, Jelly?

JELLY: He said—

JAYNE: I don't believe it, he actually—well what did he say, Jelly?

JOJO: He didn't say anything to me—

JAYNE: Me neither—

JELLY: He said, "Don't tell your sisters, but..." and then he put on his reading glasses and winked at me.

JOJO &
JAYNE: His reading glasses?

JELLY: You know, the ones he lost in—

JOJO &
JAYNE: 1967.

JOJO: *(Bitterly.)* The camping trip—

JAYNE: *(Bitterly.)* That hellish trip—

JELLY: Well the joke is, he had them all along.

JAYNE: Bastard.

JOJO: And I got the blame.

JELLY: Me too, I—

JAYNE: Yes, but I'm the one who got the blame.

JOJO: Noooo, no, no, I—

JAYNE: You were blamed for the tent pegs and I was blamed for the reading glasses, for twenty-eighty long years—

JELLY: And he told me Mr Jones—you know, Mr Jones?—

JOJO & JAYNE: *(Suddenly delighted.)* Ooooo, Mr Jones!

JOJO: And his little wee dog!

JOJO & JAYNE: Little wee dog, little wee dog!

(They giggle as of yore.)

JELLY: Well, Dad told me Mr Jones actually had three little wee dogs. And we always thought he just had the one.

(JOJO and JAYNE exchange a look.)

And he said, "Keep on with your art, Jelly."

JOJO: He did?

JELLY: He commended me my boxes and said "Don't let anything stop you."

JAYNE: Has Dad actually ever seen any of your...boxes?

JOJO: *(Discreet reprimand.)* Jayne. *(To JELLY.)* What about...did he say anything about me?

(JELLY starts to shake her head "no" then, faced with with her sister's obvious hopefulness,

reconsiders, nods "yes", and begins to fabricate.)

JELLY: He said… "Tell Jojo…do not hide your light under a bushel. You are the best professor since… Socrates."

(JOJO turns away, overcome with delight and grief.)

JAYNE: Did he…mention me at all?

JELLY: He said, "Tell Jayne…I'm sorry about the glasses, and…good luck with the…merger thing."

(JAYNE turns away, suppressing delight and grief.)

And he said, "I love you…

(JOJO and JAYNE turn to JELLY)

…all." And, "Have a good time at the party."

JAYNE: What?

JOJO: What party?

JELLY: Dad wants a party.

JOJO &
JAYNE: A party?

JELLY: Yes, and he specified, "Exactly one week from my death." And he wants us and all his friends, and he wants food and drink and step dancing and throat singing…

JOJO: Oh that's so much like Dad, it's so—

JAYNE: It's bloody weird. If we must have a party, as opposed to a reception, why can't we have it right after the funeral—

JOJO: *(Indicating Dad's room.)* Shhh!

JAYNE: *(Pouring another drink, whispering forcefully.)* Well that's how the rest of the world does it, how in the hell am I supposed to schedule a party on top of a funeral when we don't even know when—

JOJO: A week from when he dies, Jayne.

JAYNE: Yes, but when is that? I'm in D.C. on the 12th, on the 14th I open a new branch in Aspen.

JELLY: Next Friday. *(Taking a small notebook and pen from her purse, making lists.)*

JOJO: What's next Friday?

JELLY: We can have the party then.

JOJO: Jelly, Dad said a week from when he dies, not "next Friday when it's convenient for Jayne."

JAYNE: Next Friday isn't all that convenient.

JELLY: It's not all that convenient for me either.

JOJO: Jayne, Jayne, Jayne, Dad is in there dying—!

JAYNE: Shshsh!

JOJO: *(Whispering madly.)* —we have to plan his funeral, we have to plan his party. Are you trying to tell me that you're going away?!

JAYNE: My life can't just stop you know!

JOJO: Yes, yes Jayne it can, just say "Stop!" We have to make some...

                 (JAYNE protests under JOJO.)

                 We have a lot of people to— There are decisions— Jayne! Do we cremate or do we bury? Do we cook or do we cater, and what about the music?!

JELLY: It's not a lot of time, a week from today. I'll get your beds made up, the whole house needs to be cleaned—

JOJO: Jayne, I'm not saying cancel, I'm saying postpone.
               You're a bigshot, the Big Swiss Cheese, you can
               postpone—

JAYNE: Not if I don't know when.

JELLY: Friday.

JOJO: Read my lips Jelly! The party is one week from
               when he dies. We do not know—

JELLY: Yes we do.

JOJO: No we don't.

JELLY: Yes, we do!

JOJO: No, we don't!

JELLY: Yes we do, Dad said...

JOJO: Dad said, "I found my glasses," he said, "Three
               dogs hath Mr Jones," Dad said a lot of things
               among which was, "Have a party one week from
               my death!"

JELLY: That's exactly what he said, and then he winked at
               me and then he died, he's dead! I told you that but
               you never listen.

               (Silence.)

JAYNE: ...That's right, Jojo, you don't.

JELLY: So the party's next Friday and he wants us all to
               have a good time.

               (JELLY exits. JAYNE and JOJO stare into space for
               a moment, in shock. They look at one another, then
               exit together. The song, Ae Fond Kiss takes us
               into:)

Scene 2
The Funeral

(Lights isolate a bare space on the stage. JELLY enters first, dressed in a leopard-spotted raincoat. Her look is drawn downward to Dad's grave. She is joined by JOJO and JAYNE who enter arm in arm in dark raincoats, beneath the shelter of JAYNE's umbrella. JOJO weeps. JAYNE bears up. As Ae Fond Kiss progresses, each sister gradually looks away from the grave and "sees Dad". Each becomes a child again and enacts a fragment of a happy memory with their father. [There are no props other than the umbrella].)

JELLY: *(Reaching up.)* Up Daddy, up. *(Stepping onto Dad's feet, gently dancing with him.)*

JOJO: *(Opening a beloved book.)* Oh Dad…*Treasure Island*.

JAYNE: *(Closing her umbrella and casting off as though it were a fishing rod.)* I got one.

(The moments come to an end, the sisters see one another again and resume their positions at the graveside, arms around one another. For once they are perfectly close and still. JAYNE and JOJO exit, pausing to look back once. JELLY stays behind and has a moment with Dad. She feels a light kick within her belly. She smiles, then exits slowly.)

Scene 3
The Living Room

(JOJO and JAYNE enter briskly, if somewhat stunned. Their smiles and light rapid manner belie an explosive underlying tension.)

JOJO: I hate lawyers.

JAYNE: I abhor lawyers.

(JELLY crosses and stops in the doorway. She fumbles with a sheaf of documents. JOJO and JAYNE smile at her a moment too long. JELLY exits. JAYNE pours two drinks.)

JOJO: You know, Jayne, I never thought I'd say this, but owning a house and some property is the best thing that could happen to anyone.

JAYNE: *(Handing JOJO a drink.)* It's the best thing that could have happened. You know, Jojo, if Jelly hadn't just inherited the house, we'd be signing it over to her right now.

JOJO: Oh Jayne, I wish Dad had left me the house just so I could give it to Jelly.

(Shared forced chuckle. They drink. JELLY crosses, and exits carrying a large package of Pampers and a pair of baby shoes.)

JAYNE: She looks a bit pale.

JOJO: Really? I think she looks good, she's put on a little weight.

JAYNE: Looks good on her.

(A beat.)

JOJO: Good old house.

JAYNE: Wonderful old piece of shit.

JOJO: *(Chuckling.)* Oh Jayne—

JAYNE: *(Chuckling.)* —Wha—?

JOJO: Do you remember the time you flooded the whole house? When you flushed that troll down the toilet?

> *(They laugh uncontrollably, they laugh a little too long. Finally:)*

JAYNE: You know, Bertram always reminded me of that troll. *(Genuine warmth.)* How is Bertram?

JOJO: *(No longer laughing.)* Oh, you know. We see each other once every two weeks, we have a pleasant dinner followed by rather awkward sex and I don't know why I'm with him.

> *(A guffaw from JAYNE, followed immediately by embarrassed silence when she realizes her gaffe. JAYNE opens her briefcase. JOJO opens a book. After a beat, another attempt at genuine conversation.)*

How is...work?

JAYNE: Great, excellent. They've given me Mergers and Acquisitions.

JOJO: Great.

JAYNE: Yeah, slice 'n dice, lift and separate. ...How's school?

JOJO: Not too bad. Quite great. Excellent in fact. I've got one or two bright lights this year and I got my grant.

(Blank look from JAYNE.)

For my book.

(Blank look.)

On Brecht.

JAYNE: *(Sincerely enthusiastic.)* Oh, another Brecht thing, eh?

JOJO: *(Stung.)* No. It's the same old thing. It's an ongoing thing. It's highly theoretical. I don't think you would understand.

        (A beat. JAYNE, stung, pretends to work, JOJO pretends to read.)

JAYNE: I saw Cliff the other day.

JOJO: *(Choking on her drink.)* You—saw…?

JAYNE: He says hi.

JOJO: He does, does he…? How did he, how is he…?

JAYNE: He's getting a few laugh lines but he's still got that boyish—

JOJO: You ran into him?

JAYNE: No, we had lunch.

JOJO: You had lunch?

JAYNE: Yeah, once every couple of weeks we get together, have a somewhat pleasant lunch followed by rather awkward sex.

        (JOJO is shocked. JAYNE laughs.)

I got you.

JOJO: *(Laughing.)* Oh Jayne, you little devil, you got me good.

(JELLY enters with a stack of cardboard boxes.)

JAYNE: Oh Jelly, let me help you with those.

(JAYNE and JOJO attempt to take the boxes from JELLY over her inarticulate protests. A minor scuffle, then:)

JELLY: No Jayne, don't! It's for an installation.

JAYNE: Oh, what are you installing?

JOJO: An art installation, Jayne.

JAYNE: Oh. Sorry—I—so, you have a show?

JELLY: Yes, I do it's in Munich. *(Painstakingly.)* It's in the National Kunstwald Hoch Gallerie in Munchen.

(JOJO and JAYNE exchange a polite but bewildered look and watch as JELLY moves about the room struggling with increasing passion and enthusiasm to explain her art to her sisters. JELLY's text in this instance is always somewhat improvised but ends in the same way every time.)

There's a—southern exposure with a room and a box overhead and feathers that fall—floof from the—when the heat activated—from the sun and— oh, over here there's a—I take these boxes and I fill them with little clay—lives, little secret lives and you're in—and me and we and there's a hole with a—voyeuristic—and in the middle! Oh in the middle there's a row of boxes attached with a vein-like thread, a family vein and the lids open and shut and open and shut and— *(Overcome by a fit of coughing, and suddenly aware of her sisters' blank looks:)* …it's in Munich.

JAYNE: Do they pay you for that?

JOJO: *(Too pleasant.)* Must you always ascribe a cash value to everything, Jayne?

JAYNE: *(Too pleasant.)* Jelly, these are—very—well gosh, they're challenging.

JOJO: *(Desperately.)* Let's have a toast.

            (JAYNE pours drinks, JOJO hands one to JELLY.)

            To Jelly, the Homeowner.

JAYNE: To Jelly, the Artist.

JELLY: To us three in this house together again. To Daddy.

JOJO &
JAYNE: To Dad. *(JAYNE is a tad acid; JOJO, weepy.)*

JAYNE: Aren't you going to drink, Jelly?

JELLY: Oh I'm not drinking these days.

            (JELLY exits with her boxes. JAYNE pours JELLY's drink into her own. JOJO stares after JELLY for a moment, then turns to JAYNE.)

JOJO: Are you thinking what I'm thinking?

JAYNE: I was thinking about mutual funds.

JOJO: "Not drinking these days"? *(JOJO shoots JAYNE several knowing looks. JAYNE doesn't catch on.)* Oh come on Jayne, what do you think that means?

JAYNE: …She's an alcholic! A recovering alcoholic.

JOJO: *(Giving up on JAYNE.)* "I stand amazed and know not what to say—"

JAYNE: —What?—

JOJO: —C'est trop—

JAYNE: —Speak English, I never understand a word you—

JOJO: —Je m'en foux—

JAYNE: *(Spotting JELLY crossing past the doorway.)* Jelly, the market's going to get worse before it gets better, so don't be in a hurry to sell.

JOJO: Sell?! Why would she sell?!

JAYNE: *(Casually, enjoying JOJO's alarm.)* Of course she'll sell in a year or two.

JOJO: We can't sell this house—!

JAYNE: Not "we", it's Jelly's house.

JOJO: How can you talk about selling this house—

JAYNE: It's just bricks and mortar—

JOJO: Every nook and cranny is redolent with memory and meaning. Jayne, Jayne, Jayne, right here on this very spot, you took your first steps, your first little baby baby baby Jayne steps. And over here, here's where you cracked my head open when we were playing Heathcliff and Catherine. *(They share a chuckle.)* And here! Here's where Dad did his famous Beowulf recitation and Mrs Gray nearly peed her pants laughing! And right over here, we three danced for the Glee Society in matching tam-o'-shanters, *(Singing and dancing.)* "I'm a' roamin' in the gloamin'—

JOJO &
JAYNE: *(JAYNE joins in.)* with a lassie by my side."

          (JELLY enters.)

          Ohhhh, and this is where I got ma-a-arried! *(Laughter turns to sob.)* And somewhere in this house...are Mum's pearls.

          (A beat. At the mention of the pearls the moment turns quiet, tender for each sister.)

JELLY: I'm not going to sell the house. I might convert it to a drop-in centre for...people. Put a greenhouse in the attic.

(JOJO and JAYNE exchange a look.)

I'm going to need some money. *(Taking her notebook from her purse—more lists.)*

JAYNE: *(Pleasant.)* You want us to invest in your…drop-out thing?

JOJO: *(Pleasant.)* Jelly, we are each inheriting twenty thousand—

JAYNE: More like twenty-five grand.

JOJO: That's right, so—

JELLY: No, for the party. We need to decide how much money we can spend before we know how many people to invite.

JOJO: Oh.

JAYNE: The party.

JELLY: Dad's party.

JOJO: Oh Jelly, invite the regulars—oh just invite everyone.

JELLY: Did Dad ever reconcile his differences with Mr Burbury?

JOJO: Invite everyone but Mr Burbury.

JAYNE: *(Burbling in her drink, doing Mr Burbury's gooey English accent.)* Oooo, Mistah Buhboory, "Helloah girls."

JOJO: *(Giggling, burbling in her drink.)* Mistah Buhboory.

JELLY: Mrs Gray has already called.

JAYNE: *(Sharply.)* Not Mrs Gray.

JOJO: *(Pouncing.)* Why not? Why not Mrs Gray, Jane?

JAYNE: *(Instantly changing the subject.)* And whatever you do, not Mr Jones.

JOJO & JAYNE:	Oooo, Mr Jones and his little wee dog, little wee dog, little wee dog—! *(Laughing.)*
JELLY:	So I'll need quite a bit of money.
JOJO:	Charge it to our estate, dahling.
JELLY:	There's something funny about the money—
JAYNE:	You know what I'm going to do with my cut? I'm going to waste it.
JOJO:	*(Merrily.)* I'm going to hoard mine in my mattress and when I'm dead they'll find me—
JELLY:	Excuse me, ding dong, ding, there is no money.
JAYNE:	…Yes there is, Jelly.
JOJO:	There must be thousands of—
JELLY:	There's only seventy-five dollars according to Dad's bank book.
JAYNE:	*(Amused.)* More like seventy-five thousand, Jelly.
JOJO:	*(First hint of concern.)* Jelly, what are you doing with Dad's bank book?
JELLY:	Because I'm the—
JAYNE:	Jelly, why don't you just go get the bank book.
	(JELLY searches her purse, a bit too thoroughly. Then:)
JELLY:	*(Exiting.)* It's in the kitchen.
JOJO & JAYNE:	*(Reassuring one another.)* In the kitchen.
	(Crashing sounds of pots and pans, dishes, cupboards.)
JAYNE:	*(Hollering over the racket.)* Jelly? Why do you have Dad's bank book? Why do you have Dad's bank

book?!

JELLY: (*Re-entering, still searching.*) Because I'm the Attorney of Power.

> (*JAYNE and JOJO suppress their horror. Throughout the following, JAYNE and JOJO become more and more pleasant until they explode.*)

JOJO: That makes sense, Jayne. She was looking after Dad and I'm sure there were bills, but Jelly, could I just please see the bank book?

> (*JELLY searches everywhere.*)

JAYNE: This is like the time Jelly lost Mum's pearls.

JOJO: This is exactly like the time Jelly lost Mum's pearls.

JAYNE: That's why I said it.

JELLY: Here it is.

JOJO: Let me see it.

> (*JOJO and JAYNE both run and grab for the bank book, JAYNE wins.*)

JAYNE: Give it. (*Examining it.*) Well, obviously there's been some sort of computer glitch.

> (*JOJO grabs the bank book and examines it.*)

JELLY: There were expenses, you know.

JOJO: (*Through clenched teeth.*) There are twenty-nine pages of debits here, Jelly.

JELLY: I paid for things. There were medical expenses...

JAYNE: OHIP.[1]

JELLY: What?

JAYNE: OHIP!

JELLY: And a little bit of a small claims court with the male nurse and the trouble I had.

JOJO: You were sued by a nurse?

JELLY: I had to let him go… It was all settled out of court.

JAYNE: *(Fake nice.)* Jelly, where's the money?

JOJO: Jayne, calm down. *(Fake calm.)* Jelly, where's the money?

(Rapidly, hysterically repressedly pleasantly:)

JAYNE: Jojo, don't over-react—

JOJO: I'm not over-reacting—

JAYNE: Yes you are—

JOJO: I'm just I'm trying to ask a simple question—

JAYNE: You've never asked a simple question in your life.

JOJO: Would you let me handle this, please?

JAYNE: No, you know I'd like to handle it because you know this is what I do every day at work, I get paid a lot of money to do just this—

JOJO: Well I took a workshop on this kind of thing just last week—

(Vying to get to JELLY, each trying to block the other's way. JELLY tries in vain to get a word in.)

JAYNE: Goodness, a workshop, that's very impressive, but do you know what I have, *(Suddenly savage:)* I have an *MBA*—

JOJO: I think I understand the psychology of poverty—

JAYNE: I understand the psychology of wealth—

JOJO: I think I understand Jelly—

JAYNE: I think she's my sister too—

JOJO: Yes, but I'm the eldest—

JAYNE: I will handle this—

JOJO: Jayne I will handle this—

JAYNE: No you can handle the next one, I'm going to handle this one—

> (*A scuffle ensues as they continue to jabber at and over one another until, together, they turn on JELLY in a fury:*)

JOJO &
JAYNE: Where's the money!

> (*JELLY collapses backward into a suddenly reclining chair. She struggles to extricate herself while the battle rages above her. JOJO and JAYNE are fit to be tied.*)

JAYNE: Way to go, Jo—!

JOJO: Jayne, you have gone completely hysterical—!

JAYNE: You have spittle forming at the corner of your mouth—!

JOJO: Your eyes are bulging out of your face—!

JAYNE: You have a pulsating rope in your neck—!

JOJO: —and your eyebrows are going winga-winga, your blood pressure's giving me blood pressure, I was going to go back to India with that money!

JAYNE: Oh Jojo, don't dredge that up!

> (*JELLY goes to exit.*)

Jelly, Jelly, Angela, (*Roaring.*) little Jelly Bean!

> (*JELLY winces and stops in her tracks. JAYNE, suddenly calm, slips her a wad of bills.*)

Here's a few bucks for the party.

JOJO: Jayne! Jelly! Jelly, here, wait, here, where's my purse—

JELLY: I'm not stupid, you know.

JAYNE: *(Terribly kind.)* We know that, Jelly.

JELLY: Well I'm not.

JOJO: *(Terribly kind.)* Oh Jelly, we know that you're very special—now here's a whole bunch of loonies.[2]

> *(JELLY exits, first the wrong way, then the right way. JOJO and JAYNE watch and wait until she's out of earshot, then they settle in for 'A Talk', united once again.)*

Well...I knew she was a few loads short of a... *(Realizes her mistake.)*

JAYNE: *(Nodding in agreement.)* Well, it's astonishing.

JOJO: How could she be so negligent?

JAYNE: It's not negligence, Jojo, she can't help it.

JOJO: Well it is irresponsible.

JAYNE: Don't make a moral judgment.

JOJO: She is just so childish.

JAYNE: She is not childish, she is clinical.

JOJO: Jayne, don't call her clinical, she's your sister!

JAYNE: Don't you trash her one minute, then turn around and get all sucky, "Oh Jayne, you're so mean." I am sick of being the bad guy, I have done more for Jelly than—where have *you* been?

JOJO: Where have *I* been?! I don't even live here. You live in the same city as she. Why have you not been watching her?!

JAYNE: Well what am I supposed to do? Follow her around in a fake beard and glasses?!

JOJO: Yes! You know how she throws money around, often quite literally.

JAYNE   God only knows where that money went.

           (They begin to pace.)

JOJO: For all we know she could have bought seventy-five thousand copies of the *Outrider*[3]—

JAYNE: Seventy-five thousand magic markers.

JOJO: Seventy-five thousand minutes on *Speaker's Corner*[4]—

JAYNE: Seventy-five thousand cardboard boxes—

JOJO: Maybe she spent it on her art.

JAYNE: You call that art?

JOJO: You're such a philistine.

JAYNE: I pay taxes!

JOJO: Just because she's an artist—

           (They stop and confront one another.)

JAYNE: Van Gogh was an artist! *(Pronounces it Go.)*

JOJO: Van Gochch! *(Pronounces it gutterally.)*

JAYNE: You're disgusting.

JOJO: You have always been jelly of Jealous. If you were only more honest with yourself.

JAYNE: I am not jelly of Jealous!

JOJO: You sublimate and project, you have never had a significant other.

JAYNE: Put away the Freudian cattle prod, Jojo you're a nutbar, you should be in therapy—

JOJO: I am in therapy!

JAYNE: Because you are extremely fucked up!

JOJO: No...(*Suddenly calm again.*) Jelly's fucked up.

JAYNE: ...Yeah.

(They exit, and a clap of thunder takes us into:)

Scene 4
Living Room (The Past)

(Sounds of a storm. Night. JELLY, the child, dashes on, in her nightgown, crying hysterically. She hugs her teddy bear and clutches the long strand of pearls. She stares, sobbing, at the window.)

JELLY: Mum? Dad?

(JAYNE, the child, enters sleepily, wearing pyjamas.)

JAYNE: Jelly? Jelly Bean?

JELLY: Jayne...I'm scared.

(JOJO, the child, enters, nightgowned, putting on her glasses, waking up.)

JOJO: What are you two doing up?

JAYNE: Come away from the window Jelly. Mummy and Daddy will be home soon.

JOJO: Don't worry, Beanie. They're out dancing and having fun.

JELLY: I'm scared they're dead.

JOJO: *(Amused.)* Oh Jelly, they're not dead. What time is it Jayne?

JAYNE: *(Amused.)* It's four in the morning.

JOJO: *(Horrified.)* Four in the morning?!

JELLY: You see? They're dead.

JOJO: Jelly, they are not dead. Dad is...an excellent driver.

JELLY: *(Sobbing.)* Mu-um?! Da-a-ad?!

JOJO &
JAYNE: *(Sobbing.)* Mu-um?! Da-a-ad?!

JOJO: Oh God!

JELLY: Do you think that they're angels yet?

JAYNE: I'm gonna throw up.

JOJO: Oh don't worry, little Jelly Donut.

JELLY: *(Crying.)* We'll be orphans, and we'll have to live in a box!

JAYNE: I can't breathe!

               (JELLY and JAYNE clutch each other.)

JOJO: Breathe, Jayne! *(Pledging:)* If Mum and Dad are dead—which they are not—we'll stay right here. We'll all live together in our beautiful house, *(Choking up.)* and I promise you, my dear sisters, we will never, never go to an orphanage. I will cook and clean and I will read aloud every night.

JAYNE: I'll get a job!

JELLY: I won't bite, please make them not be dead and I will never bite!

JOJO: I will never marry.

JAYNE: We'll have a dog.

JELLY: And a snake.

JOJO: I swear by Mum's pearls.

JAYNE: By Mum's pearls.

JELLY: Mummy's pearls.

(They each take reverent hold of the pearls, caress their cheeks with them and sigh, comforted. Then giggle wickedly.)

JOJO: But you will both have to remember that I am the eldest.

JAYNE: Yeah Jelly, no more telling on us if they're dead.

JOJO: Jayne, they're not dead.

JELLY: Yeah, Jayne!

JAYNE: Don't worry, Jelly, they're not really your parents anyhow, they just found you one day in an old packing crate and decided to keep you in case they got hungry.

JELLY: No they didn't!

JAYNE: "No they didn't!"

(JAYNE starts tickling JELLY, seizing her by the wrist and making her slap her own face with her own hand. JELLY laughs and whines at the same time.)

JAYNE: Stop hitting yourself, Jelly.

JOJO: Cut it out, Jayne.

JAYNE: She likes it.

JELLY: I like it. Ow! Stop it, Jayne!

JOJO: I'm going back to bed.

JELLY: Wait up! Jojo, can I sleep with you in your bed?

JOJO: *(Indulgent.)* Oh all right, Jelly.

(They begin to exit.)

JAYNE: You guys, no fair!

JOJO: Oh Jayne, you can come too.

(JOJO joins her sisters at the exit, and JELLY runs off. JOJO pulls JAYNE back and whispers briefly in her ear. They giggle wickedly and instantly transform into scary creatures, limping and lurching off after JELLY.)

JOJO &
JAYNE: *(Scary whispers, exiting.)* Jelly! Ohhhh Jelly!

Scene 5
The Kitchen (The Present)

(Morning. JELLY, dressed for the day, enters, turns the radio on at full volume, dances, makes tea and transforms the living room into the kitchen by means of a large kitchen table, colourfully set for breakfast. This scene has a light rapid rhythm on the surface, but is driven by an underlying tension fed by JOJO and JAYNE, that boils over by the end. JAYNE enters in robe and slippers, talking on her cell phone.)

JAYNE: I know what Merrill Lynch said and what I'm saying is there's a direct feed from the Minister's office to the *Financial Post*— *(Turns down radio.)* If they acquire Corel, big if— *(JELLY hands JAYNE a cup of tea.)* No, Steve, Steve, I can't be there— I told you it's a family thing... Of course I have a family.

(JAYNE sits at the table. JOJO enters dishevelled in her robe, slippers and dark glasses, carrying a portable backrest, blowing her nose and leaving a trail of Kleenex. She heads for the table.)

JOJO: This house is freezing. Why is it always so cold? I was never warm a day in my life in this house. My whole childhood was one long torture chamber.

(JOJO sits. JELLY pours her a cup of tea in a high arc. JOJO chokes up.)

Oh Jelly, you did that just like Mum.

JAYNE: *(Into phone.)* Look Steve, here's something that'll help you—

JELLY: *(To JOJO.)* Would you like a jelly donut? I made them myself.

JAYNE: *(Into phone.)* —their CEO's booked in for a penis extension.

JOJO: Did you sleep okay, Jelly? I didn't sleep a wink. Every time I dozed off I started marking papers and cleaning squid—

         (JELLY turns the radio up a little.)

JAYNE: I'm serious, focus on that when you walk in, you'll be fine.

JOJO: —and then I'd wake up exhausted, soaking wet, I'm probably going into early menopause. I thought I had ten, maybe fifteen more years. Jelly, do you think I will die childless?

JELLY: *(Embarrassed.)* I don't…know…Jojo.

         (JELLY exits, picking up JOJO's Kleenex as she goes.)

JAYNE: *(Into phone.)* I'll fax you the numbers— *(Chuckling.)* Yeah, I love you too, you scum-suckin' fuck-ugly sonofabitch. *(Hangs up.)*

         (JOJO turns on a tape: Pachelbel's Canon in D Major.*)*

         'Morning, Jo. You look great.

JOJO: Well I feel terrible. I didn't sleep a—

         (JELLY re-enters with a hot water bottle for JOJO.)

JELLY: I feel great. I got a lot of work done last night.

JAYNE: Didn't you go to bed?

JELLY: No, I worked, I have a big show coming up in—

JAYNE: You look terrible.

JOJO: She looks fine.

JAYNE: She looks feverish, that's insomnia.

JELLY: I don't have insomnia.

JOJO: I have insomnia.

JAYNE: *(Patting JELLY's hand.)* Jelly, if you go without sleep for extended periods of time with no ill effects it means you are running on pure endorphins.

JOJO: Excuse me, Doctor Kildare, when did you get your MD?

JAYNE: I read widely. Contrary to what you might think.

JOJO: A little knowledge is truly a dangerous thing.

                 (JOJO and JAYNE share a fake-pleasant chuckle.)

JELLY: I felt a little sick this morning, but I'm fine now.

                 (JELLY exits. JAYNE returns to her newspaper.)

JOJO: This morning? Felt sick this morning?

                 (JOJO stares after JELLY and clears her throat meaningfully at JAYNE, who is oblivious.)

                 Jayne.

JAYNE: What.

JOJO: *(Whispering.)* I think she is.

JAYNE: What?

JOJO: *(Whispering.)* I think she's…you know.

JAYNE: No, what?

                 (JOJO mimes pregnancy. JAYNE finally catches on.)

                 You think she's pre—

(JOJO sees JELLY coming and throws the hot water bottle at JAYNE to silence her. JELLY enters with her purse. JOJO and JAYNE "act natural". JELLY picks up on the Pachelbel's Canon which is still playing, and sways appreciatively, eyes closed, while JAYNE and JOJO try to sneak a peek at her abdomen.)

JELLY: Ahhh. Taco Bell's Canon.

(JOJO and JAYNE exchange a look.)

JAYNE: What did you call it, Jelly?

JELLY: Taco Bell's Canon.

JAYNE: That's what I thought you said.

(JAYNE laughs behind her paper, JOJO laughs in her tea.)

JOJO: It's...Pachelbel's *Canon*, Jelly.

(JELLY chuckles—she knows she's right. JOJO and JAYNE are convinced she's loony. Phone rings. JELLY answers.)

JELLY: Hello?...Oh hi Mr...yes, any time between four and nine. We're having the cake at eight...yes, yes you can. You can bring your grandchildren...It's all right Mr Burbury, you don't have to talk so loud.

JAYNE: Mr Burbury?

JELLY: No, Mum won't be here...

JOJO: Jelly, why did you invite Mr Burbury?

JELLY: Mum's dead, Mr Burbury...yeah, ten years ago—

JAYNE: Jesus Murphy.

JELLY: Yuh, any time between four and nine...yuh, at eight...okay...yes, yes you can bring your grandchildren, yuh…any time between four and nine…that's right…yes, yes, between four and nine…yuh…yuh…yuh, between four and nine…at eight. (*She repeats it all louder and louder until she manages to hang up.*)

JAYNE: Jelly, why is Mr Burbury—?!

JOJO: (*Drooling impression of Mr Burbury.*) Mistah Behbooorryy.

JAYNE: Grow up, Jo. (*Switching off tape.*) Jelly, Mr Burbury is incontinent. He peed on the couch last time—

JELLY: He's one of Dad's oldest friends, we'll put down plastic.

             (*JELLY takes out her notebook and pen: more lists and checks. The phone rings. JELLY answers.*)

             Hello?…Oh, just a minute. (*To sisters.*) It's the Physics Department from Dad's university, there's fifteen of them, think we can handle it?

             (*JOJO and JAYNE indicate "no". JELLY shakes her head "no" in agreement, returns to phone.*)

             Sure.

             (*JOJO and JAYNE, exasperated. Phone rings. JAYNE grabs it.*)

JAYNE: Hello! (*Disguising her voice.*) No-o-o-o, this is…Catrina, this is not Jayne, here is Jelly.

JELLY: Hello?

JOJO: "Catrina"?

JELLY: Oh, hello Mrs Gray.

JOJO: Grow up, Jayne.

JELLY: Between four and nine, cake at eight…great, thanks for resevepeeing. (*Hangs up.*)

JOJO: I haven't seen Mrs Gray since Mum's funeral.

               (JAYNE hides in her newspaper.)

JELLY: Mrs Gray's a lesbian now.

JOJO: Really? Isn't she a little old for that?

               (Phone rings. JELLY answers.)

JAYNE: I'm not here.

JELLY: Hello?…yes…oh, I don't know. *(To sisters.)* What should we write on the cake?

JAYNE: What cake?

JELLY: Dad's cake.

JOJO: Do we really need a cake?

JELLY: *(Exasperated.)* There's always a cake. *(Into phone.)* Just put…" Goodbye George". …Yeah…Uh-hum. *(Hangs up.)*

JOJO: Where's my purse? This house is like a mythological sea monster, it devours things. I can never—

JELLY: *(Taking out her notebook.)* Jojo, did you bring your car?

JOJO: Yes, Jelly.

JELLY: Can you get the cake?

JOJO: Of course, Jelly, I'd love to, just as soon as I've had a little lie-down.

JAYNE: You can't sleep, we have to clean the house for the party.

JOJO: Don't worry Jayne, I'll call Mrs Crowe.

JAYNE: What for?

JOJO: To clean the house.

JAYNE: That's why we're here. That is why I took the day off work, so I could work, don't you dare go back to bed.

JOJO: Am I the only one not in denial?

             (JOJO takes a "self-massager" from her purse—wooden balls strung on a rope, with wooden handles at either end—and starts massaging her own shoulders.)

             There has been a death in the family. We have been bereaved. I for one could not sleep. I for one need time to grieve—

JELLY: It's good to grieve, Jojo, I'll send a taxi for the cake—

JOJO: I'll get the cake, Jelly, it's just—I keep getting these waves— *(Teary.)* I know this sounds Freudian, but I dreamt I was carrying Dad's head last night and he kept saying—his head kept saying—"Don't drop me! Don't drop me!"

JAYNE: For someone who didn't sleep a wink, you sure had a lot of dreams. Who are you calling?

JOJO: *(Dialling.)* Mrs Crowe.

             (JAYNE disconnects JOJO's call. JOJO grabs JAYNE's cell phone and is about to dial, but there is someone on the line.)

             Hello? Oh, yes, just a moment. *(To JAYNE.)* It's for you.

JAYNE: Yeah Steve, what do you want?…Oh, hi Caroline—

             (JAYNE turns away for privacy. JOJO and JELLY eavesdrop.)

             Fine…well yeah…well, me too. *(Sexy chuckle.)*

(JOJO and JELLY accidentally draw attention to their eavesdropping.)

I can't talk right now…No…I don't know…I know. Look, I'll call you. *(Hangs up.)*

JOJO: Is there something wrong at work, Jayne?

(JAYNE shakes her head, "no".)

She sounded worried.

JAYNE: *(Roaring.)* Jojo!

(JOJO jumps. JELLY's newspaper, or whatever she is holding, takes to the air.)

With all your fake Marxist bleeding heart pseudo-feminist liberal Brechtianism, you are perfectly willing to exploit that poor woman.

JOJO: Who?!

JAYNE Mrs Crowe!

JOJO: For God's sake, Jayne, Mrs Crowe worked for Mum and Dad for twenty years—

JAYNE: She's old, leave her alone!

JOJO: Jayne, that is ageist. Just because she's old you don't have to ship her off to the glue factory. Mrs Crowe likes to work, "I like to verk, I like to verk!"

JAYNE: How can you be so racist?

JOJO: Racist?! Mrs Crowe is white!

JAYNE: Do you know what her real name is?

JELLY: Her real name is Krakokokoscevics.

JAYNE: *(Still oblivious to JELLY.)* It's Krakokokoscevics. In her day that meant something. She was a minority.

JELLY: Albert Einstein was once a minority.

(Neither JOJO nor JAYNE register JELLY's interjection. JAYNE barrels through.)

JAYNE: Do you know why we have a democracy, and what remains of a free market system?—

JELLY: "God does not play dice."

JAYNE: —It's because people came from all corners of the globe and they weren't ashamed to work. I am not ashamed to work. *(Grabbing a cloth, scrubbing.)* See? I am working and I'm looking for my inner child all at the same time, I am new age, I am woman!

JOJO: Jayne, maybe if you could just feel your grief—

JELLY: *(Standing on a chair, trying in vain to get their attention.)* I'd just like to say that ninety-five people have RSVP'd and they're all expecting cake.

> *(JELLY gives up. She cleans up the breakfast table, occasionally getting caught in her sisters' crossfire. JOJO and JAYNE ignore her until they roar at her. Even then, they keep their eyes on one another.)*

JOJO: Jayne, when Bertram left—I mean, when Cliff left, I went on this housework binge—

JAYNE: Do you know why Cliff left?

JOJO: I don't have to listen to this.

JAYNE: Because you never listen!

> *(JOJO bursts into tears.)*

Classic avoidance technique!

JELLY: I've got a doctor's appointment in half an hour—

JAYNE: Jelly! That is why so few women get to where I've got, they're in the grips of one long PMS!

JELLY: I'm getting an ultrasound—

JOJO: Jelly! Tell Jayne that I feel sorry for her, I feel even sorrier for her than I felt for Cliff, and Cliff was truly the numbest individual—

JELLY: I don't know if I want to know if it's a girl or a boy—

JAYNE: Jelly! Tell Jojo that I can't stand to be around her negative, negative—she is like a dwarf star or something, everything implodes around her—!

JELLY: I was hoping you guys would be happy.

             (JAYNE can't breathe. She puts a hand over her heart.)

JOJO: Oh, oh my phantom limb, oh my palpitations—having another "stroke", Jayne?

JAYNE: Jojo, I am sick to death—!

JOJO: As am I!

             (Telepathic moment between JOJO and JAYNE. Very funny, but deadly serious as they read one another's minds.)

JELLY: Auntie Jo and Auntie Jayne.

JOJO: *(Grave.)* Are you saying our lives would be better if we didn't see each other ever again?

JAYNE: *(Clenched.)* I'm saying we haven't seen each other much in the past few years, and perhaps we ought to continue the trend.

             (JELLY gives up and exits.)

JOJO: Fine.

JAYNE: Fine.

JOJO: It's not like much will change.

JAYNE: That's right.

JOJO: Let's just try to be civil until after the party.

JAYNE: And once the party's over...

> (The phone rings but JOJO and JAYNE ignore it and turn away from one another, convinced their relationship is over. JELLY enters and answers the phone.)

JELLY: Hello? Oh hi, Mr Jones.

> (JOJO and JAYNE instantly turn to one another:)

JOJO &
JAYNE: Ooooo, Mr Jones and his little wee—

> (They catch themselves and turn away again.)

JELLY: Between four and nine, cake at eight. (Hangs up.)

JOJO &
JAYNE: Jelly, why did you invite Mr Jones?!

JELLY: He once gave me a box of seeds.

> (JOJO and JAYNE exchange a look. JELLY exits. Music and lights cue the transition. JOJO and JAYNE, with rapid precision, transform the space into the attic, never forgetting for a moment that they are at war.)

Scene 6
The Attic

(The attic door opens and JELLY enters, wearing a crinolined party dress in splendid colours. A beat. She takes in the attic, then speaks, softly at first.)

JELLY: Dad? Mum? It's a girl. Another little Fine girl. I wasn't going to ask or look at the ultrasound, but I couldn't resist. And the timing has worked out well because for the show in Munich I'll be six months along, and that's optimum field-plowing bear-wrestling time for pregnant women, and all I have to do is talk about my work...

(It occurs to her that this might be harder than plowing a field. JELLY begins to explore the attic and the contents of its trunks.)

Oh and don't worry about Jojo and Jayne. They'll come around.

(Finds the torture dress and tambourine.)

Or maybe they won't.

(Among other things, she finds Dad's old tuxedo jacket that JAYNE wore in the Prologue, and finally comes across a cardigan of Mum's: a treasure. Music. She buries her face in it and breathes in.)

Oh Mum.

(She puts on the cardigan to feel its embrace and puts her hands in the pockets. A beat. She has found something. Out from one of the pockets she pulls a long strand of pearls. Amazement and joy. JAYNE,

*dressed for the party, emerges through the attic
door, talking on her cell phone. She doesn't see
JELLY. Over JAYNE's first line, JELLY moves to
greet her and show her the pearls but stops herself,
at first because she doesn't want to interrupt, and
then because she is caught in the awkwardness of
having heard more than she ought. JELLY pockets
the pearls and hides.)*

JAYNE: Hi Caroline darling, it's me…fine—well the party
            hasn't actually started yet…No…yeah I, think this
            party could go on all night… No…Gosh, you know
            I'm pretty sure I'm in Houston that night…well I'm
            not at all certain we should see each other
            again…no, I—it—it isn't— I am not scared! I'm
            listening…Oh don't say that…yes…yes…of course
            I did, you're— I think you're beautiful… Because I
            can't. —Look, don't do this to me, don't put me in
            this position— *(She's been hung up on.)* Shit.

            *(JELLY attempts a quick escape but JAYNE turns
            in time to catch her. JELLY freezes.)*

            …That was a client.

JELLY: I know Jayne, I wasn't listening.

JOJO: *(From below.)* Jaaayne…Jellyyy!

            *(At JELLY's instigation, she and JAYNE hide as
            JOJO enters cautiously, laden with a tray of forks
            and napkins. JELLY and JAYNE leap out at her
            with a cry, JOJO screams and her tray goes flying.
            JELLY and JAYNE laugh.)*

            What in God's name are you two doing up here?

JELLY: Look, I found the torture dress—

JAYNE: What are you doing up here?

JOJO: Looking for you two. We have guests arriving any
            second.

JAYNE: Jojo…

JOJO: *(Snaps.)* What?

JAYNE: …Nothing.

JOJO: I thought so.

JELLY: *(Fondly.)* Remember when we used to play up here? Remember when we'd put on dress-ups and dance and have tea parties and tell secrets and you guys would never let me wear the torture dress? Remember when you used to fill up buckets of water for me to swim in, and one was the Atlantic Ocean and one was the Pacific? And how you'd lock me in the trunk and pretend I was an old doll you found that used to belong to some dead girl? Remember the time I bit you and you let me wear Mum's pearls?

> *(JOJO and JAYNE are tempted to say "yes", but catch one another's eye.)*

JOJO &
JAYNE: No.

JELLY: You guys. *(Patting her pocket where the pearls are.)* I have a surprise for you.

JOJO: *(Gasp!)* It's all right Jelly, Jayne and I know—

JELLY: You do?

JAYNE: Know what?

JELLY: How could you possibly know?

JOJO: Well a sister just knows these things. *(To JAYNE.)* Unless she's completely insensitive.

JAYNE: *(Getting it.)* Ohhh! Jelly, sweetheart, bottom line here, are you going to keep it?

JOJO: Jayne!

JELLY: I thought we could share it.

JOJO: That's quite an assumption, Jelly.

JAYNE: Whose is it, Jelly?

JELLY: It belongs to all of us. I thought we could divide it
                equally in three—

JAYNE: Jellly, I will help with money but I am not the type
                to—

JELLY: *(Pulling out the pearls, unnoticed by JOJO and
                JAYNE.)* Oh Jayne, it would look great on you.

                *(The doorbell rings. JELLY pockets the pearls again.
                No one moves to answer the door.)*

JAYNE: You better get down there.

JOJO: Why me?

JAYNE: Well I'm not getting it.

JOJO: Afraid it might be Mrs Gray? What's she got on
                you anyway, Jayne?

                (The doorbell rings again.)

JELLY: Jojo, please answer the door.

JOJO: Why me, pray tell?

JAYNE: You're the eldest.

JOJO: Why doesn't Jelly get it?

JAYNE: Yeah Jelly, it's your house, you get it.

JELLY: Let's all get it.

JOJO: Yes Jelly, let's all get it. For one last time let's be a
                family; for one last time let's rise above rancour
                and betrayal, injustice, lies and little murders; for
                one last time let's march down those stairs without

a backward glance and greet our guests like the three Fine girls we are. Let's do it for Dad. *(Exit.)*

JAYNE: Let's do it for Mum too. *(Exit.)*

JELLY: Let's do it for... Four. Four Fine girls. *(Exit.)*

(Rapid transition. JAYNE re-enters immediately through the attic door, giggling, wearing an oversize lady's hat and jacket from the 50s, and we are in:)

Scene 7
The Attic (The Past)

(JOJO follows JAYNE immediately, likewise dressed up. They sip from imaginary teacups, giggling prissily yet somehow wickedly. After a brief moment:)

JELLY: *(From below.)* Wait for me!

(JELLY, in dress-ups including her yellow pointy bra, and carrying a small box, joins them.)

JOJO: How lovely to see you, Mrs Gray. Tea?

JAYNE: Oh Mrs Fine, I would love some tea.

JELLY: I want to play Mum.

JOJO: Jelly, you are Mrs Burbury.

JAYNE: *(Drooling Burbury accent.)* Mrs Bluhbluhrry.

JELLY: I don't wanna be Mrs Blabla.

JOJO: Sandwich?

JAYNE: Oh yes, I would like a sandwich very much.

JELLY: *(Grabbing.)* Oh yes, I would like a sandwich too.

JOJO: How is your sandwich, Mrs Gray?

JAYNE: Oh Mrs Fine, it is a lovely *(Choking.)* poison sandwich!

JOJO: Ah ha! That means you're the devil himself!

JAYNE: No, I am not the devil, I am a vampire!

(JOJO and JAYNE attack one another and JELLY gleefully, JELLY laughs and screams.)

JOJO: Die Prince of Darkness, die!

JELLY: Wait, no, okay, I wanna, wait, okay, okay, I wanna, I wanna...I wanna—no—okay, okay, no, I wanna—I— *(Continues in this vein until JOJO and JAYNE are thoroughly disgusted, then:)* I wanna play hunt the thimble, and I'm a snake!

JOJO: No, we're going to play Little Women and I am womanly Meg and you are my troublesome sisters whom I love more than anything, my darlings.

JELLY: I wanna play hunt the thimble!

JOJO: Jelly, you have to do what I say 'cause I've got my period.

JAYNE: I'm gonna barf! *(Exit.)*

JOJO: Oh Jayne... Oh. I'm going to go read a book. *(Exit.)*

JELLY: *(Bursting into tears.)* I wanna period toooo! I don't even know how to read a book!

(JELLY wails and howls a series of semi-comprehensible threats and grievances, mostly to do with how Dad is going to savagely punish JOJO and JAYNE on her behalf. At first her upset is real, but soon she begins to enjoy the sound of her own sobs which eventually turn into laughter. She picks up her small box and shakes it vigorously. She opens it and takes out a Barbie head on the end of her finger. She bites the head off, laughs and shakes the box with the head inside it ever more vigorously, until she hears party music from below.)

(Delighted.) A party?! Wait for me! *(Exit.)*

Scene 8
Living Room (The Present)

(The party is in full swing. Wild 50s party music. JOJO enters, carrying a tray of martinis, nervous and hospitable. JAYNE enters carrying a tray of oysters.)

JOJO: Jayne, where's Jelly?

JAYNE: *(Smiling for the guests.)* I'm not speaking to you.

JOJO: Jayne you've got to help me, Mr Jones is all over me.

JAYNE: Tough titty.

JOJO: Oh Jayne, don't be so immature—oh no, here he comes, dance with me!

(JOJO grabs JAYNE and dances with her. Calling over her shoulder:)

Sorry Mr Jones, my dance card is full.

(They dance on.)

JAYNE: Cliff is looking for you.

JOJO: Cliff?!

JAYNE: Cliff.

JOJO: *(Over JAYNE's shoulder:)* Oh Mrs Gray, care to cut in?

JAYNE: *(Breaking away, heading for the exit.)* I'll kill you.

(JAYNE escapes, crossing JELLY who blows on a party noisemaker.)

JOJO: *(To JELLY.)* Where have you been? *(Calling to offstage.)* Oh no, Mr Burbury, not the couch! *(Runs off, followed by JELLY.)*

Scene 9
The Attic

> (*JAYNE enters with a glass of Scotch. She takes a sip. Then another. And another. Then she drains the glass. She catches sight of herself in the mirror.*)

JAYNE: I look great. I'm almost forty and I look...I look fine. Mrs Gray. And who is your young friend? Your under-aged, over-educated neo-hippy girl...thing with the woven...everything. (*Removes her jacket.*) You're living on an organic free-range vegan woman's farm now? That is fascinating. (*Undoes a button on her shirt.*) That's better. (*More buttons.*) That's good. (*Opens her shirt to reveal her bra.*) I should just go down there like this, there's nothing wrong with this. (*To Mrs Gray.*) Oh I see various people, but you know you can't net a high six figures and commit. Not that I'm a workaholic. (*Spots the torture dress.*) I know how to have fun.

> (*The attic door opens and JELLY's head pops in. She sees JAYNE in her bra, purring and growling with the torture dress, and retreats.*)

I play games...of chance!

> (*JELLY peeks in again and is nearly spotted by JAYNE:*)

I windsurf! And I can talk about books too, you know, I read that *Fall on Your...Fugitive...* thing.[5] Oh Mrs Gray. Are these the breasts of a workaholic?

> (*JAYNE squeezes her cleavage together, leans forward into the mirror, and spots JELLY behind her. JELLY withdraws instantly, closing the door, JAYNE struggles frantically back into her clothes, then seconds later, JELLY enters as though nothing had happened.*)

JELLY: Hi Jayne.

JAYNE: Is it time for cake?

JELLY: Jayne, (*Crossing to a trunk.*) do you want the torture dress?

JAYNE: The—? Of course not, Jelly, what on earth would I do with it, what are you looking for?

JELLY: Music for Mr Burbury and Mr Jones. They're going to do a barbershop duet.

JAYNE: Quartet, Jelly if I wanted the dress I would take it, you wouldn't have to give it to me. Besides, Jelly dear, don't you see, it's not yours to give.

> (*JAYNE opens the door to exit but is confronted by JOJO poised in the doorway, brandishing a large cake knife.*)

JOJO: I just want to know why, Jayne.

JAYNE: Why what?

JOJO: Why did you invite Cliff to the party?

JAYNE: Why not?

JOJO: He is my ex-husband, Jayne...*ex*!

JAYNE: So? Cliff knew Dad, he was part of the family.

JOJO: Was, was! That's what divorce means, Jayne!

JAYNE: Well I didn't divorce him.

JOJO: Far from it.

JAYNE:	I thought we weren't talking.
JOJO:	We're not.
JAYNE:	Fine!
JOJO:	Fine!
JELLY:	You guys—
JOJO:	*(Snaps.)* Jelly, we know you're pregnant!
JELLY:	No, I know you mean—but I didn't think, when you—that's not what I—
JAYNE:	Jelly, spit it out!
JOJO:	Jayne, drop it.
JAYNE:	Why are you always protecting her?!
JOJO:	Why are you always on the attack?
JAYNE:	Me?!
JOJO:	You treat her like a nincompoop.
JAYNE:	It is a scientifically proven fact that the brains of pregnant women shrink!
JOJO:	Jayne!
JAYNE:	I read it in *Maclean's*.[6]
JOJO:	Quit deflecting, Jayne, you're always deflecting and denying, deny, deny, deny, you're the Queen of denial. Now. I am going out to the shed to get the cake and when I return I expect Cliff to be gone.
JELLY:	You guys—
JOJO:	Not now, Jelly, I have to get the cake.
JAYNE:	Then go, why don't you!
JELLY:	Jojo, do you want the torture dress?

JOJO:	The what? Of course not, Jelly.

(JELLY goes to exit with the dress.)

JAYNE:	Jelly, it's not yours to give.
JOJO:	That's true, sweetie, it isn't.

(JELLY thrusts the torture dress at JAYNE, who takes it. JELLY exits.)

JAYNE:	Aren't you going to get the cake, Josephine?
JOJO:	You must be relieved. Mrs Gray seems to have forgotten all about you.
JAYNE:	*(Quietly.)* When did you turn into such a bitch?

(JAYNE exits, leaving JOJO genuinely stung. JOJO allows herself to break down, then spies something in a trunk. A glittering and very long silk scarf. She rushes to the trunk, picks up the scarf and embraces it passionately, reverently. Music. Lights. JOJO is back in India. She is young once more. She is with her first love, Oomesh. Throughout the following text, as her memories become wilder and more erotic, she improvizes a dance that is both comical and sincere. She moves, undulates, winds and tangles herself up in the scarf until finally she stumbles to the floor.)

JOJO:	Oh Oomesh. My first and only love. Oomesh. I never thought I'd leave you. I never thought I'd leave India. Oh Oomesh, how do you say "Kiss me" in Hindi? How do you say "Threepenny Opera"? We are each other's destiny. Destiny is India and India is destiny. Oh Oomesh, lie naked with me in the mango groves.

(The attic door inches open, hands reach out toward JOJO who stares in horror. This is JOJO's nightmarish memory in which JAYNE's voice wheezes and echoes:)

JAYNE: Jo-o-o-Jo-o-o…Jo-Jo-o-o-o…

              (Door closes)

JOJO: *(Reliving the dreadful memory.)* Oomesh. I must go.
              It's my sister, Jayne. She's ill, she needs me, she's—
              oh Oomesh! Jayne… Don't die, *(Sobbing.)* Jayne,
              please don't die, I've come home, sweetie, I've
              come back…Jayne!

              *(Burst of evil laughter as the attic door flies open.
              JAYNE wearing the torture dress and shaking the
              tambourine, laughs at JOJO, then abruptly
              disappears behind the door again. JOJO is crushed
              and shaken. Party sounds resume below, signalling
              the end of the nightmare. JOJO carefully returns the
              India scarf to the trunk. Then she picks up her cake
              knife and, out for blood now, exits through the attic
              door. Party music gets louder and takes us into:)*

Scene 10
The Party

(JAYNE enters, tipsy, a drink in one hand, cell phone in the other. She dials and speaks into the phone:)

JAYNE: Hi Caroline angel, baby, darling, it's me.

(JELLY enters with a tray of jelly donuts.)

JELLY: Jayne, have you seen Jojo? It's way past eight and still no cake.

(JOJO enters with her knife, and heads for JAYNE.)

JAYNE: *(On phone.)* Don't hang up!

JOJO: *(Grabbing JAYNE's phone.)* Hi, Caroline? Is your refrigerator running?

(JAYNE laughs at first, then JOJO closes the phone. JAYNE and JELLY are shocked.)

(Deadly, to JAYNE.) Don't you have a closet to clean out somewhere?

(JOJO tosses the phone to JAYNE. JAYNE catches it and crumples. JOJO triumphantly spears a jelly donut from JELLY's tray with her knife and brandishes it.)

JELLY: Jojo, it's a party! Dad's party!

(JELLY spots JAYNE trading in her glass for a bottle of Scotch.)

Jayne!

(*JAYNE exits one way drinking from her bottle,
JOJO exits the other way with her donut and knife.
JELLY is left, torn. She follows JAYNE.*)

Scene 11
The Attic

*(JAYNE enters, drunk, clothing awry, to a burst of
Macarena from below. She falls spectacularly, but
saves her bottle. JELLY enters.)*

JELLY: Jayne, the line dancing has started and it was your
           idea—

JAYNE: Jelly—I can't—breathe.

JELLY: Oh Jayne, not now.

           *(JAYNE begins to panic, muttering "There's no
           breathing happening here, no breathing whatso-
           ever". JELLY goes to her.)*

           Jayne, Jayne put your arms up—keep your clothes
           on Jayne!—arms up—up, that's it.

           (JELLY tickles JAYNE who laughs and gulps air.)

           Okay!

JAYNE: *(Laughing.)* Yeah! Whoo!

JELLY: *(Laughing.)* Whoo!

           *(Over the following, JAYNE laughs and dances the
           Macarena, JELLY joins in.)*

JAYNE: Jelly, am I a bad person?

JELLY: Well Jayne...we're all...a bit bad.

JAYNE: I know but I think I'm bad, you know...bad. Like
           just now. In the kitchen. With Cliff.

(*JAYNE macarenas her way through an explicit grinding kiss she laid on Cliff, then stops to gauge JELLY's reaction.*)

Am I bad?

JELLY: Well you're not really bad, Jayne, you're just…not normal.

JAYNE: What's that supposed to mean?

JELLY: I don't mean not normal is necessarily bad, Jayne. I'm not normal and I'm fine, maybe you're not normal too and that too could be fine.

(*JAYNE stares at JELLY for a dangerous beat.*)

JAYNE: Jelly. I love you.

JELLY: Thank you Jayne.

JAYNE: I don't love anything else. You're the only thing I love.

JELLY: You love your work.

JAYNE: I don't love my work.

JELLY: You love your client.

JAYNE: (*Embracing JELLY, tickling her.*) Jelly, you're my only little sister and I wuv you! What do you want? Hey? I wanna buy you somethin'.

JELLY: I don't want anything, Jayne.

JAYNE: I wanna buy you a boat!

JELLY: I just want to go back to the party.

(*JELLY takes JAYNE's hand. JAYNE is cheerfully rubber-legged. A pas de deux as JELLY attempts to exit with JAYNE and JAYNE remembers to take her bottle with her. JAYNE stops, suddenly savage:*)

JAYNE: Who is that with the earring in her eyebrow?!

JELLY: Who?

JAYNE: Who is that down there?!

JELLY: That's Mrs Gray's young friend, Joni.

JAYNE: Ha.

JELLY: She makes jewellery.

JAYNE: I'll bet!

JELLY: She does.

JAYNE: Do you know why, Jelly?

JELLY: Because she's a jeweller?

             (JAYNE gasps at the sight of something behind JELLY. JELLY gasps in turn. JAYNE crosses to a trunk and tenderly lifts out an old tigerskin coat.)

JAYNE: Jelly, I have a confession to make.

JELLY: Oh Jayne, please, I don't want to know anything, I already know everything and I don't want to know anything.

JAYNE: *(Kneeling.)* Oh God I wish I were Catholic— It was ten years ago at Mum's funeral reception, right here in our house. Jojo was playing *Tales from the Vienna Woods* on the piano, she had just served the cake. Nobody suspected that, meanwhile... upstairs—

JELLY: I know Jayne. I saw you and Mrs Gray on the coats.

             (A beat. JAYNE gapes at JELLY.)

             My room was being used as the coatroom as usual and I came in to get a box and I saw you and Mrs Gray...

             (JELLY briefly does a discreet but unmistakable physical impression of what she witnessed.)

...on the coats. So I got my box and I left.

(A beat. JAYNE continues to stare. Finally, smiles.)

JAYNE: Jelly. I was a bit drunk a minute ago, but I'm better now and I need your advice.

JELLY: My advice is go back down—

JAYNE: If a person loves another person. And the other person loves that person back. But the person who loves the person back tells the person they love that they don't love them. And tells them to go away. Well. What do you think?

JELLY: Jayne, who are you talking about? Yourself?

JAYNE: Yuh.

JELLY: And...your client?

JAYNE: My... *(Breaks down and cries.)*

JELLY: *(Embracing her.)* Oh Jayne, my advice to you is...quit your job, move to country with Caroline, have a garden, Jayne, have dogs, and babies or—be happy Jayne, just be happy.

            (JAYNE looks up, wipes her eyes and puts on a smile.)

JAYNE: Would you like anything from the party, Jelly? Any pickles, or ice cream?

            (JAYNE heads for the exit with her bottle and tigerskin coat.)

JELLY: Jayne.

JAYNE: Yes Jelly?

JELLY: Jayne...I love you.

JAYNE: *(Breezy.)* Thanks Jelly. *(Exit.)*

            (JELLY is crushed and at a loss. She takes out the pearls and comforts herself with them.)

JELLY: Mum? Dad? I've got an idea for a new box. It'll be quite plain except for the words painted in large authoritative letters, "Danger. Do Not Open." Or "Open Verboten"—'cause the show's in Munich. And it's empty. The only empty box. Some people may not open it. They'll just stare at it, wondering, "What is so dangerous to me that I dare not open it?"

                (JELLY puts the pearls back into the pocket of Mum's cardigan, then takes off the cardigan and puts it back into the trunk where she first found it. She closes the lid of the trunk, then discovers that the hem of her dress is caught. She tries to open the trunk but the lid won't budge. Her struggle with the trunk has become noisy and almost hysterical when JOJO enters with her cake knife, dazed and seemingly oblivious to JELLY's racket. JELLY sees JOJO after a moment, and pauses in her panic to free herself. JOJO sits and stares into the void.)

                Hi Jojo.

JOJO: *(Noticing JELLY for the first time.)* Oh Jelly, it's you. Hi.

JELLY: Hi. How are you?

JOJO: Fine. How are you?

JELLY: Fine. I guess.

JOJO: What's wrong?

JELLY: I'm stuck. Could you help me?

JOJO: Oh goodness, of course. *(Moves toward JELLY but stops.)* I can't.

JELLY: What do you mean you can't?

JOJO: I don't know. *(Chuckles.)* I can't seem to do anything right now.

JELLY: That's terrible.

(JOJO tries to let go of her knife. JELLY joins in the effort, demonstrating how JOJO should simply open her hand. Finally the knife flies out of JOJO's hand toward JELLY, who screams.)

JOJO: You could say I'm on a holiday.

JELLY: Where are you?

JOJO: On a holiday.

JELLY: Yes, but where? India?

JOJO: Don't be silly, Jelly. I'm in the attic.

JELLY: Yes, that's true.

             (Beat.)

JOJO: *(Tearful.)* You look just like Mum.

JELLY: That's nice.

             (JOJO moves toward a trunk.)

             Jojo, are you having a nervous breakdown?

JOJO: No Jayne, nothing like that.

JELLY: It's Jelly.

JOJO: I had no idea this was up here.

             (JOJO pulls out her wedding gown from the trunk and struggles into it.)

JELLY: Dad put it here after your divorce.

JOJO: What did you say Jayne, I mean Jelly?

JELLY: Nothing.

JOJO: I'm just having a bit of a hard time at the party.

JELLY: How's that?

JOJO: Oh, people are looking at me funny.

JELLY: What do you mean, funny?

JOJO: Oh, you know, they're just looking at me funny.

JELLY: Well, I guess I don't know—

JOJO: They're looking at me funny!!

JELLY: I'm sorry.

JOJO: No, I'm sorry Jelly. I'm really sorry because *(Bursting into tears.)* Igagethegake.

JELLY: What's that?

JOJO: I can't get the cake! Oh Jayne!

JELLY: It's Jelly.

JOJO: I've tried several times to go to the shed to get the cake and every time I get to the door, somebody or something gets in the way.

JELLY: You mean—?

JOJO: For example Cliff. Every time I'm on my way to the shed, Cliff walks by.

JELLY: Well you could just keep going past Cliff to the shed—

JOJO: And then when I pass through the living room everyone looks at me with expectant eyes as if to say "Where's the cake, Jojo? You're the eldest, Jojo. Why aren't you more like your mother, Jojo? Where's Bertram, Jojo? Don't you have children yet, Jojo? What, still no tenure, Jojo? I'm hungry, Jojo. Where's the cake, Jojo?!"

JELLY: Oh Jo.

JOJO: *(Weeping.)* I'm sorry if I've failed everyone but I can't be like Mum and I can't get the cake.

JELLY: Yes you can, Jojo.

JOJO: Why can't they eat bread, for God's sake? *(Cries.)*

JELLY: Jo, it's a very simple thing. You just have to go back downstairs and pretend that you're lighter than air and float past all those eyes, past Cliff, past Bertram…

JOJO: Bertram's not here yet. Cliff is. Cliff is here. For some reason Cliff is here.

JELLY: Then float through the kitchen door, through the trees and into the shed.

JOJO: Through the trees and into the shed.

JELLY: And get the cake.

JOJO: And get the cake.

JELLY: And float back to the house.

JOJO: And float back to your house.

JELLY: And put the cake on Mum's rose petal plate.

JOJO: The rose petal plate.

JELLY: And cut it.

JOJO: And cut it!

JELLY: And then serve it.

JOJO: And then serve it.

JELLY: On napkins!

JOJO: On napkins! *(JOJO works herself into an enthusiastic frenzy, then:)* How ridiculous. Of course I can get the cake. *(Leaving.)*

JELLY: Jojo. Could you help me now?

JOJO: Jayne. I mean Jelly. I just want to say that I'm very excited about you being—you know—pregnant.

And that you shouldn't worry about me being—
you know—not pregnant.

(Gathering the train of her gown, leading with her knife, JOJO exits.)

JELLY: *(In despair.)* Jojo! Jayne! Someone!

Scene 12
The Party/Attic

(Roamin' in the Gloamin' plays. *JAYNE enters the party wearing a tam-o'-shanter, and the tigerskin coat open to reveal bra and boxer shorts. She is covered in lipstick kisses. She swigs from her bottle and cruises the audience. JOJO enters in wedding dress and matching tam-o'-shanter, wielding her knife. JAYNE intercepts her. They circle one another. JAYNE lays down her bottle, JOJO lays down her knife and they square off, then break into the Highland Fling. The Fling devolves into other dances—ie. Charleston, Bump, Monkey, Twist—they are oblivious to JELLY's first cries from the attic.)*

JELLY: Help. Help. Help. HELP!

              (JOJO and JAYNE stop, look up at the ceiling, then at each other.)

JOJO &
JAYNE: Jelly!

              (JAYNE grabs bottle, JOJO grabs knife and they run off.)

Scene 13
The Attic

(JOJO and JAYNE enter, fighting to get to JELLY first.)

JOJO &
JAYNE: Jelly, are you all right?

JELLY: I'm trapped— *(She wails incomprehensibly.)*

(JAYNE and JOJO somehow free her from the trunk. JAYNE removes her coat revealing her bra and boxer shorts beneath, and puts on the tuxedo jacket from the Prologue.)

JAYNE: Jelly, what were you doing playing up in the attic all by yourself?

JELLY: I was not playing—

JAYNE: Well I think we should all be present if there's going to be any sorting—

JELLY: Look, if you want anything you can have it, take everything—

JAYNE: I just think we should catalogue the entire—I don't want anything, but I want to attach a value to everything.

JOJO: Oh Jayne, we're not going to go through every piece of costume jewellery, every old scarf—

JAYNE: *(Tossing the India scarf at JOJO.)* Oh you can have all the old dead scarves.

(*JOJO and JAYNE glare at each other. They look like refugees from the top of a wedding cake.*)

JELLY: What if Mum's pearls turned up here?

(*A beat. They all soften.*)

JOJO: When Mum died I wanted them to magically turn up.

JAYNE: Those pearls were always disappearing.

JELLY: And reappearing…

JAYNE: Jojo…do you remember the time you lost Mum's pearls?

JOJO: …Oh Jayne, how could I forget?

(*The following section is improvised. The pace is rapid and the story that JOJO and JAYNE relate to each other and to JELLY is fragmented because they both know it so well. They laugh throughout and the audience should pick up only on key words and phrases until the end. The story: one night years ago, JOJO snuck home at three in the morning from a date, only to discover that she had left Mum's pearls behind at her boyfriend's dorm. She woke JAYNE up to drive her back to the dorm and on the way they kept veering off the road due to JAYNE's opthomological palpitations. When they got there the dorm was locked so JOJO climbed the trellis. They were laughing really hard at the time and JAYNE thought it was raining, but in fact JOJO peed on her head.*)

You thought it was raining—

JAYNE: (*Overlapping with above.*) I thought it was raining—

JOJO: And I peed on your head !

JAYNE: You peed on my head!

(*All three are overcome with laughter.*)

JELLY:	You what?
JOJO:	She thought it was raining—
JAYNE:	And she peed on my head! Oh Jojo, who was that guy, who was your boyfriend at the time, was that Cliff?

(JOJO stops laughing. JAYNE and JELLY notice and likewise stop, a bit bewildered. JOJO addresses JAYNE, quietly furious.)

JOJO:	It was Oomesh. You know perfectly well it was Oomesh. That was the night I decided to go with him to India and give up my apprenticeship with Lotte Lenya and the Berliner Ensemble. Blissfully unaware that six months later I'd be on a plane back home, abandoning everything I'd ever loved, heeding the call to your supposed deathbed.
JAYNE:	Jelly, would you please tell Jojo—
JELLY:	No.
JAYNE:	What did you say?
JELLY:	You two are so juvenile.
JAYNE:	We're juvenile?!
JOJO:	Jelly, I find it a teensy bit ironic that you're lecturing us on immaturity—
JAYNE:	Who's the father?!
JOJO:	Jayne, don't pry.
JELLY:	There isn't one.
JOJO:	Jelly, there must be a—oh dear, maybe your brain *has* shrunk—
JELLY:	He's a donor. There's a difference.
JAYNE:	A Jelly donor.

JOJO: Well what do you know about him?

JAYNE: It was the male nurse, wasn't it, the one who sued you.

JOJO: Jayne, male nurses are gay. Jelly, if you want us to help you—

JELLY: I don't want any help—

JOJO: An unemployed single welfare Mother—

JELLY: I'm not unemployed—

JAYNE: A child is having a child.

JELLY: I am not a child!

JAYNE: Yes you are.

JELLY: No I'm not.

JAYNE: Are so.

JELLY: Am not!

JAYNE: Are so.

JELLY: Am not!

     (They repeat this until JAYNE tickles JELLY and makes her slap herself with her own hand. JELLY protests and laughs by turns.)

JAYNE: Stop hitting yourself, Jelly. Stop hitting yourself.

JELLY: Ow- hahaha—Ow!

JOJO: *(Outraged.)* Jayne, stop it!

     (JAYNE gives JELLY a raspberry on her belly, JELLY shrieks with laughter, JOJO winds up and wallops JAYNE on the bum with the tambourine.)

JAYNE: Ow!

JOJO: Jayne, you are a really bad influence on Jelly, why

do you think she's so screwed up?! It's because you have a weird relationship, it's weird what you do with her. I—I can't talk about you and Jelly, I get all fumbly because it's weird, and—I must say it once and for all.

JAYNE: What.

JOJO: That you have a weird relationship and it's...

JELLY: Weird?

JOJO: *(To JAYNE.)* Well one minute you're beating her up and the next you're all kissy, smoochy, mwa mwa—

JAYNE: Are you saying that our relationship is sexually perverse?

JOJO: I, I, I was—not thinking of sex, I was not—

JAYNE: Well what do you mean by weird?

JOJO: Why has Jelly never had a significant other?

JELLY: I've had several relationships with several men—

JOJO: Promiscuity is a symptom.

JAYNE: Of what?

JOJO: ...Confusion.

JAYNE: That's ridiculous. *(To JELLY.)* I sleep with tons of people and I'm not confused.

JOJO: Jelly is confused thanks to you, why do you think she flirts with old men like Mr Jones?

JAYNE: Jelly, is he the father?

JOJO: Oooo.

JAYNE &
JOJO: *(For each other.)* Oooo!

JAYNE: Jelly, if he touched you—Jelly...were you abused as a child?

            (A beat.)

JELLY: Yes.

            (JOJO and JAYNE: aghast.)

            (To JAYNE.) By you!

JAYNE: What?—

JELLY: "Oh Jelly, come into my bed, little Jelly", tickle, tickle, then pound, pound, pound!—

JAYNE: Ow!

JOJO: It's true, Jayne.

JELLY: *(Turning on JOJO.)* "Mum and Dad are dead, Jelly!" *(To both.)* Jelly, oh Jelly, come right this way little Jelly, that's right, right into the dryer! *(Relives the horrifying motion of the dryer.)* I was not flirting with Mr Jones! I was just being nice to him in a way he understands. Don't you ever do that?

JAYNE: No.

            (JELLY, disgusted, goes and sits in a trunk.)

JOJO: *(To JAYNE.)* Ha! "Oh Mrs Gray, how's the dog breeding? That's a lovely bunch of grapes you're wearing, step into my closet, right this way through the revolving door!"

            (A beat. JOJO and JAYNE lock eyes. JELLY watches them nervously.)

JAYNE: *(Casual.)* Cliff.

JOJO: ...What do you mean..."Cliff"?

JAYNE: Cliff, Cliff, Cliff, that's all just Cliff.

            (A dangerous beat. Cat and mouse:)

JOJO: I know you slept with Cliff. Didn't you.

JAYNE: If you know…why are you asking me?

JOJO: Why don't you admit the truth for once?

JAYNE: I have no secrets.

JOJO: You have nothing but secrets.

JAYNE: I guess that makes me…interesting!

            (The scene speeds up:)

JOJO: It makes you pathetic! There is nothing wrong with
            being a lesbian, Jayne! A lot of women would give
            their eye teeth to be gay, to have real intimacy with
            someone as nurturing and sensitive as oneself, I'd
            probably have tenure by now if I were a lesbian, in
            fact sometimes I wish I were a lesbian.

JAYNE: Jojo, are you telling me you're a lesbian, it's all
            right, I always thought you were.

JOJO: I am not a lesbian!

JAYNE: Well why not if it's so warm and fuzzy?!

            *(JAYNE gasps, clutches her heart, staggers. JOJO is
            casual at first:)*

JOJO: Do you fake everything, Jayne? Or just your spells
            and your phantom limb and your palpitations? Go
            ahead, Jayne, have a heart attack, have a lovely
            infarction, lie down and fibrillate, if you can.
            (Losing it.) Fibrillate, fib!

            *(JAYNE collapses in a spasm. JOJO stands over her,
            furious.)*

            I had to come home from India because of your
            fucking stroke and it was just a bad case of pins and
            needles! Just a bad case of Mrs Gray! I hate you!

            (JAYNE lies perfectly still.)

Jayne, get up now. Jelly, go call an ambulance.

JELLY: What's the number?

JAYNE: *(Weak.)* Jo...

JELLY: *(Singing softly, trying to remember.)* Nine six seven...eleven, eleven...[7]

(JOJO bends to JAYNE and tenderly cradles her head.)

JOJO: What, Jayne?

JAYNE: ...he said...

JOJO: Who said—what said who, Jayne?

JAYNE: Cliff...he said...*(JOJO leans closer.)* He said..."Oh Jayne... Oh...Jayne." *(Grinding her hips.)* "Ohhhh Jayne!"

(JOJO is apoplectic, JAYNE scampers away, delighted.)

He said the problem was you didn't understand him. When men say that it means only one thing. You wouldn't go down on him!

(JOJO grabs a cane and gives chase. JAYNE screams in terror of JOJO and tries to use JELLY as a shield. Clothes and fur fly. JELLY tries desperately and in vain not to get caught in the middle.)

JOJO: You can do better than that, Jayne. Come on! Torture me some more! *(Brandishing the torture dress.)* Put it on, Jayne, it's your turn. *(Throws dress at JAYNE.)* Put it on! *(JAYNE struggles half way into the dress.)* Oh. You can't. You're too fat.

(They're both laughing.)

JAYNE: Jo, let's not do this.

JOJO: Have you been eating too many pastries to sublimate your sexuality?

JAYNE: *(Laughing.)* Let's go get the cake.

JOJO: *(Laughing.)* Oh it's pastry time, is it? Nothing like a fat lesbian!

JAYNE: I'll kill you.

                (Fight. Strangulation. Hair-pulling. No holds barred, venomous and hilarious. JELLY finally succeeds in breaking it up.)

JELLY: Stop it! Stop it! We have guests, this is not what Dad wanted!

JOJO: *(Turning on JELLY.)* Don't lecture me on what Dad wanted!

JELLY: Dad said—

JOJO &
JAYNE: "Dad said!"

                (The following is rapid and insane as JOJO and JAYNE, by now already right around the bend, gang up on JELLY who tries to explain. JOJO is enraged to the point of tears.)

JOJO: I am sick and tired of your special relationship with Dad, I came into this house first, Jelly Fine!

JAYNE: And I came second!

JELLY: Give me the torture dress, I want to do the torture!

JAYNE: Babies can't torture.

JELLY: I was here for a year—

JAYNE: *(Imitating her in a baby voice.)* "I was here for a year."

JELLY: It was me who—

JAYNE: "me who—"

JELLY: Dad was so sick—

JAYNE: "Dad was so sick—"

JELLY: It was me who, the money was—the house was
             entrusted to me—

             *(JAYNE says and does what JELLY says and does
             almost simultaneously until JELLY seizes
             JAYNE's arm and bites it. JAYNE cries out in pain.
             She and JOJO are shocked.)*

JAYNE: Jelly! No biting!

JOJO: Jelly! You must never bite!

JELLY: Listen to me—

JOJO: The only reason you got the house is because Dad
             knew you couldn't look after yourself!

JELLY: *(To both her sisters.)* Get out!

             (JOJO and JAYNE are shocked into silence.)

Get out of my house.

             *(A beat. JOJO and JAYNE are speechless. JELLY
             takes the torture dress from JAYNE and exits.
             Thunder and lightning. JAYNE exits, JOJO takes
             off her wedding dress in the shadows. The storm
             takes us into:)*

Scene 14
Living Room

> *(The wreckage of the attic has become the wreckage of the living room. Sound of rain against the windows. JOJO speaks into the phone.)*

JOJO: June? Hi. This is Jojo Fine. Just fine, thank you. Yes, I'm phoning because your father is asleep in our bathroom and I was wondering if...what's the best thing... Just leave him there? Fine... Of course he can stay there... No it wouldn't put us out. I'll keep in touch... Yes, we're fine—thanks for asking. Bye.

> *(JAYNE enters.)*

JAYNE: Mr Jones is in our bathroom. Is Jelly back yet?

JOJO: No. Are you sure she's not in the house, did you look—?

JAYNE: I've looked everywhere—

> *(They pace nervously.)*

JOJO: Did you look in all the rooms? *(JAYNE nods throughout.)* Did you look in Dad's room? Did you look in the closets?

JAYNE: I looked in the closets.

JOJO: Dad's closet?

JAYNE: I've been through all the closets... Jojo—

JOJO: Oh Jayne, you don't have to—

JAYNE: I am gay. That is...a lesbian. As of now.

JOJO: Oh Jayne, that's…very nice of you. Thank you.

JAYNE: You're welcome.

            *(Awkward beat. They beam at each other, almost
            hug.)*

            So…do you think people had a good time?

JOJO: Oh I think so—

JAYNE: They drank all the punch.

JOJO: I think all the music got played. What time is it
            Jayne?

JAYNE: It's four in the morning.

JOJO: Oh God!

JAYNE: Oh Jelly! Oh Jo, I'm gonna throw up—

JOJO: Breathe Jayne.

            *(They rush to embrace one another. Emotional and
            long-awaited. They pat each other repeatedly.)*

JAYNE: Oh Jojo, I'm sorry.

JOJO: No, I'm sorry.

JAYNE: No, it was me—

JOJO: It was me, it's always me—

            *(Thunder, lightning. JELLY enters, wet, wearing
            the torture dress and pearls.)*

JELLY: Someone left the cake out in the rain.

JOJO: Oh Jelly—

JAYNE: Oh thank God.

            *(JOJO and JAYNE move as though to go to JELLY
            but something in JELLY's manner stops them. They*

merely listen. JELLY calmly addresses her sisters.
As her text progresses, she becomes more emotional
but does not succumb to tears.)

JELLY: A respirator.
            I.V. stands.
            An adjustable bed.
            Bedpans.
            A catheter.
            Palliative care course.
            Humidifier.
            Dehumidifier.
            Morphine.
            It costs a lot to die at home.
            I took care of Dad because I wanted to.
            It was hard, but it was one of the happiest times of
            my life.
            We talked.
            I got a lot of work done.
            I hired a bicycle courier to cut the lawn.
            I got pregnant.
            I so wanted to tell you.
            I didn't know how to tell you.
            Her name is Jesse. Jesse Fine. With a J.
            I'm leaving. For Munich. There's an exhibition of
            my boxes.
            I'm leaving at dawn.
            I don't want you to phone me.
            Don't write to me.

            (A beat.)

            ...Oh, and by the way. I found Mum's pearls.

            (JELLY slowly removes the strand of pearls from
            around her neck. And breaks them. JOJO and
            JAYNE watch them scatter. JELLY exits. JOJO and
            JAYNE pick up several pearls, then exit.)

Epilogue

(Music: Ae Fond Kiss *throughout. Until the end of this scene, it must be clear that the sisters, despite their proximity on stage, are not in the same place. JELLY enters, pushing a baby carriage. She has a large manila envelope addressed to her in Munich. She hesitates, then decides to open it. Inside she finds a small box. She opens the box and takes out a tiny pearl necklace. She smiles and shows it to the baby. JOJO and JAYNE enter, each wearing an identical tiny strand of pearls. The sisters look at one another. And laugh.*

The End.)

Endnotes

1. OHIP stands for Ontario Health Insurance Plan. Substitute a local reference.
2. Loonies: the Canadian dollar coin. American productions can substitute pennies.
3. The *Outrider* is a newspaper sold by homeless people, and costs one dollar. Other productions may substitute a local reference or use the line, "seventy-five thousand pounds of jelly beans."
4. Speaker's Corner is a TV network's video booth, in which members of the public can express their opinions on camera for a dollar.
5 Book titles may be substituted. Pick any two well-known books that Jayne might want to claim she's read, then mix up the titles.
6. U.S. productions may substitute *Time* for *Maclean's*.
7. Use your local Pizza Pizza number.